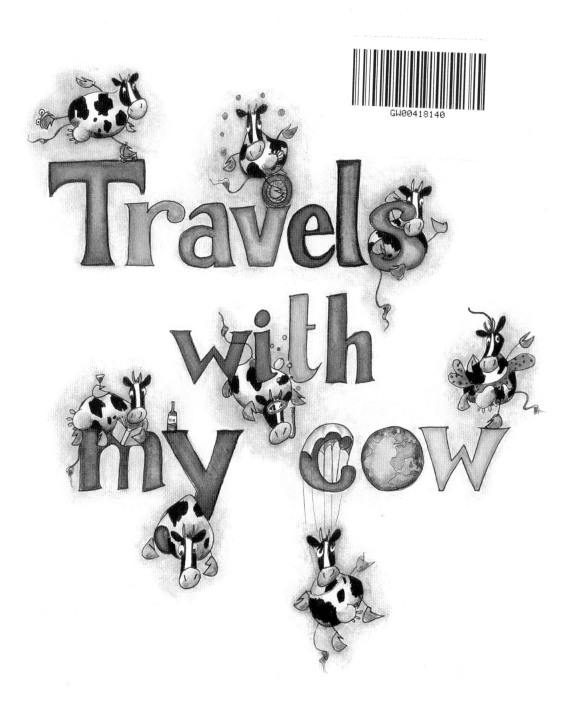

Travels with my cow

The true story of one woman's adventures around the Globe dressed as a Pantomime Cow

By Jane Silver-Corren ● Illustrated by Kate Chidley

Dear Lucy + friends!

Hope you enjoy this!

love
Janet

First published in 2006 by Smiley Books UK
The Trees, 26 Uplands, Walditch, Bridport, Dorset DT6 4LE.
E-mail: travelswithmycow@onetel.com

© 2006 Jane Silver-Corren.

Designed and printed by Creeds the Printers, Broadoak, Bridport DT6 5NL. Tel: 01308 423411

With thanks to the Western Gazette for the supplied photographs.

ISBN 10 digit: 0-9552559-0-2
ISBN 13 digit: 978-0-9552559-0-8

Front cover designed by Kate Chidley featuring photos of Worms at The Trooping of the Colour in Windsor Castle (1991), in Geysers de Tatio (1992) and with Jane.

Contents

I Wandered Lonely As A Cow

By Jane Silver-Corren (It does have a very jolly tune!)

I wandered lonely as a cow that ambles over hills and fields,
And people ask me why and how I travelled bovine between meals.
Nostalgically I will reply "I haven't really got a clue",
But it felt great to be disguised as something furry that says moo.

Chorus: Will you? Will you? Be my back end will you?
I promise not to fart or worse do anything that's too subversive
Will you? Will you? A new experience for you,
I promise not to jog or run or try to show you my bare bum.

I put the costume in my pack, the body, front legs, back legs, head.
The udders I could not fit in, so I took Marigold gloves instead.
I did inflate these, 'ere I went, and attached them to my front bum,
Then I would put the costume on and send a photo to my mum.

Chorus

And often as I drifted on, I searched for a back end to be,
A good companion for my cow and appear in the pics with me.
In Eastern Europe, Thailand. The Americas and Blighty too.
I'd put my cuddly outfit on and roam like real cows do.

Chorus

And oft times folk would shout and cheer,
And smile and wave and laugh a lot.
I found it a terrific buzz, though some would say I looked a clot.
Eventually another cow I added to make up a pair.
And at my sad old married friends posh weddings, cows in love appeared.

Chorus

And now I'm forty, o so old, my udders they sit on the shelf.
I'm much too busy to find time to gad around in my 'cow self'.
But now and then I get the urge to find a friend, get the cow on,
So then round Bridport I must roam, singing this very silly song.

Chorus. End.

Introduction

This is my life's work. My first life that is, because they do say that life begins at forty and I am about to reach that moment of rebirth. I hope it begins with chocolate milk this time round. I'll have a pint please, with a dash of Baileys.

And talking of milk, my story is about the various adventures that I have had travelling around the world, and in good old Blighty, dressed as the front end of a pantomime cow. There was always a back end, of course, but the contents of this varied depending on where I was at the time and who was available to nab.

In between the factual bits, which are illustrated by genuine on location photographs, I have indulged myself in a few little fantasies about what I would do if I was Supercow, the most talented cow in the West. Hopefully after my rebirth I will in fact become Supercow. I have been rubbing my magic udders on a regular basis. She is able to do all the things that I can't even do in the most simplistic way, and of course she does them a million times better. The amazing Kate, who just happens to specialize in drawings of Friesian cows doing incredible things, has illustrated the Supercow stories.

Obviously I hope that you'll enjoy these musings & pictures, but I also hope that they will be a source of inspiration to you. It only occurred to me when approaching my 40th birthday that these bovine travels are the most exciting thing I've done so far in my little life, so maybe I should make a slightly neater record of them. Maybe you've just reached your 40th Year & fancy a little break from the humdrum of normal life. I would highly recommend a dabble in furry costume travel. Just imagine there could be hundreds of us 40 somethings circling the globe in a wide variety of animal 'two parters'. Wouldn't that be great!

Throughout the book I refer to the Friesian cow as Worms and the Hereford bull as Snailey. Before you reach this point and become confused and mystified, I would like to offer a brief explanation. Note that on some of the photos the cows have udders and on others they are udderless. This is because they are fortunate enough to have detachable udders. The cows therefore have a choice of sexual identity-with udders female, without male, so in a manner of speaking they are hermaphrodite, rather like worms and snails, hence their chosen names Worms and Snailey. When it has become necessary to refer to gender in the text Worms is referred to as 'she' and Snailey as 'he' as these are the stereotypical roles they adopted at wedding parties. It was their idea, not mine. I would also like to explain that 'a compression pack' which is also referred to in the text, is a small, sausage shaped bag, perfect for stuffing a pantomime cow into. It has various strings attached to it to allow you to compress it into as small a size as possible. Unfortunately I have not yet met a compression pack that is large enough to fit a pair of udders as well as a cow.

I have decided that all the profits that I make from this book will go to one local charity and one national charity. Because my cow and I spent 6 months in South America we are raising funds for WAWA which supports underprivileged children & young people in Peru. The charity is very small and is run by a couple who live in Powerstock, Dorset. I am also supporting Send a Cow for obvious reasons, and I hope to raise enough to send a cow to Africa. Whilst you are enjoying this book you can be sure that the profits are being enjoyed by someone who really needs them – I would have just blown the whole lot on chocolate buttons.

This is probably a good point to say thanks; to Dan and the kids for being tolerant of my stressy moments and being supportive during the times when I had to hide away and write and type, to Charlie the parrot and to Cathie for help with editing bits, Mum & Dad for buying Worms for my 24th birthday, and for all those little old back ends out there, where ever you are.

During my 'musings and rememberings' songs just popped into my head, as they do, so I have taken the liberty of writing them down so you can sing in between

sections, a bit like a commercial break & theme tunes all rolled into one. If you don't know the original tune just make one up. I believe it adds greatly to the entire experience, even better if you moo along, but not recommended in a bus or on the train, and definitely not in the doctor's surgery.

Happy wandering through
my first life's adventure.

The Happy Wanderer by Antonia Ridge

I love to go a wandering along the mountain track
And as I go, I love to sing, My knapsack on my back.
Valderi, Valdera, Valdera, Valde-ha ha ha ha ha ha
Valderi, Valdera
My knapsack on my back.

I love to wander by the stream that dances in the sun,
So joyously it calls to me, "Come! Join my happy song!"
Valderi, Valdera, Valdera, Valde ha ha ha ha ha ha
Valderi, Valdera "Come! Join my happy song!"

High overhead, the skylarks wing
They never rest at home
But just like me, they love to sing
As o'er the world we roam
Valderi, Valdera, Valdera, Valde ha ha ha ha ha ha
Valderi, Valdera As o'er the world we roam

Oh, may I go a-wandering
Until the day I die!
Oh, may I always laugh and sing
Beneath God's clear blue sky
Valderi, Valdera, Valdera, Valde ha ha ha ha ha ha
Valderi, Valdera Beneath God's clear blue sky!

Jane and Worms.
What amazing
adventures they were
to have together...

Moo Beginnings

Please don't panic, dear reader. I am not intending to title each chapter with some incredibly naff moo-related name. I just fancied a little dabble with the moo thing in my first and last chapters. After all this is possibly the only book I am ever going to write, so why shouldn't I have a little indulgence?

Anyway, up, up and away with the story...

"Why did you decide to travel around the world dressed as a pantomime cow?" A question I am often asked.

And my reply is generally rather vague because I'm not really sure to be honest; it just seemed like a good idea at the time.

During my various musings, and whilst writing this book, I came up with a number of possible answers to this question.

A) I enjoy making people laugh and I enjoy laughing. Seeing a cow-like creature wandering round doing things a cow-like creature wouldn't generally do is funny, as is being that cow-like creature and doing those very same things.

B) I like adventures.

C) I like performing but am not fantastic at it and sometimes feel embarrassed. Being inside a cow is a great way to perform without being known, and will guarantee an audience on any occasion.

D) I wanted to meet my soul mate and had a very wierdy spooky wooky type calling, from a very friendly sounding inner voice, telling me that the way to do this was to don furry cow-like garb and wander around a lot.

E) A herd of cows in the Far East contacted me via their spirit god and invited me to join them in my next life, suggesting that the way to do this was to practise being a cow in this life.

F) When dressed as a cow, I am automatically transformed into a capable super-hero type character, that doesn't necessarily do super hero rescuing activities but just acts in a super hero type way.

G) There is possibly a genetic predisposition that creates a desire to want to dress up in animal like disguise. My youngest son Toby has wanted to go out and about dressed as a dragon since the age of 2 (he is now the ripe old age of 5 and maintains a healthy interest in his dragon gear)

And the correct answer to this question? You'll just have to read on to find out!

The seeds of my new life were planted in exotic Hounslow, November 1990, to be precise, where I was working as a publicity and press officer at a wondrous library. It was fairly wondrous as far as libraries go as it had its own café and theatre attachments. We put on a pantomime to launch the anniversary of the birth of the new look library and used the panto cast to stage a number of publicity stunts in the grand old borough of Hounslow. I decided to stage a mock hold up of local shops with Robin Hood, his merry men, and his merry horse gallivanting around the town centre holding up local shop keepers at gun point (ha ha ha, ho ho ho what a wonderful sense of humour I had in those days, only 16 years ago). It wasn't quite as exciting as the previous year's stunt when British Airways lent me Concorde. The panto cast of Dick Whittington and his cat then staged a fake disembarkation after their adventures in the Far East (sorry, couldn't resist chucking that one in as I was so proud of myself for borrowing Concorde from B.A.)

Anyway, as I was saying before I went off on my ego trip of a tangent, the publicity stunt was successful, the mayor and his wife were thrilled (glory be) and I got to borrow the pantomime horse for the weekend. It was a rather special horse, with fluttering eyelashes, fibreglass head, fur of soft velvet, hooves of gold and so on. I feel rather unfaithful to Worms for saying this, but the horse was definitely a rather more superior breed of panto creature, even with the more recent addition of upgraded pure silk udders to Worms' repertoire.

When the publicity stunt was over I eagerly sped boatward bound as I was living on a houseboat in Richmond-upon-Thames at the time. My car full to bursting with pantomime horse. This was definitely not the flat pack/easily transportable variety of pantomime creature, due to his enormous head, no insult intended to those large headed readers. My boat friend Mike and I couldn't wait to wear this trusty steed and gallop into the wilds of jolly Richmond-Upon-Thames!

We spent the evening touring the pubs of Richmond as a horse. It really was one of the most amazing evenings of my life, up until that particular point of course, because little did I know I had many more 'amazings' yet to come. Is this all rather sad and a poor reflection on my opinion of my life up until this point? Probably. Anyway, Mike wasn't quite so enthralled by the experience, which was possibly due to his role as back end of the horse. As well as having the disadvantage of not being able to see anything, by the end of the evening he had developed acute backache. Still he was fairly cheerful, considering, and particularly enjoyed those moments when we had to escape to the nearest loo in horse disguise and emerge a few minutes later as human beings. I suppose we were a bit like superheroes, but with the slight disadvantage of having to try to conceal a large fibreglass horse head and other bulky furry bits in rather small loos. No I don't mean actually in the loo, I mean in the toilet facility area. Thanks particularly to the White Cross for its large Ladies Conveniences.

Oops, I nearly forgot to describe what was so amazing about the whole being a horse thing. In a nutshell, it was the general reaction from onlookers. A mixture of disbelief, wonder, and laughter, lots of laughter, sometimes quite hysterical. I particularly enjoyed the 'disappearing superhero' bits at the end of each visit, though wasn't quite so enthralled with the 'trying to sneak the costume out of the pub' bit after we'd had a drink or two. It was fascinating to sit at the bar listening to people's reactions. I felt like a superhero, superstar and very amusing person all rolled into one happy, eyelash flashing, furry parcel.

Fired up with my newfound enthusiasm for pantomime creatures, I spent many happy moments chatting to the pantomime Dame from Robin Hood in between performances. She was a terrific source of inspiration, because as well as possessing literally hundreds of pairs of frilly knickers, she owned two pantomime cows & two panto horses. She put me in touch with a pantomime costume retailer in Eastbourne, Gaytime and Gala, and within days I went up to Eastbourne by train to collect my very own costume. It felt like an important occasion and I wanted to see the entire selection on offer. I really enjoyed perusing the various choices on the list they sent me, but my final choice, the Friesian cow, must have been a one-off. He was not featured on the original publicity, and was the only Friesian in stock. I was very tempted by a rather friendly looking giraffe, but, on reflection, this would have been an unfortunate choice, as the neck would not have easily fitted into a compression pack & therefore would have been very tricky to travel around with. Just in case you fancied popping into Gaytime and Gala and making your own purchase, I am sorry to say that the shop closed down shortly after I bought Worms. I suppose there isn't a huge demand for adult fancy-dress costumes.

Sing A Merry Song anon.

Sing a merry song as you stroll along
Though your song be short or very long
Sing it high or low, sing it soft or strong
But sing a merry song
Sing a merry song, sing a merry song
  as you stroll a long, long, long
Sing a merry song, sing a merry song,
  as you stroll along

Moo a merry song as you move along
Though your song be short or very long
Moo it high or low. Moo it soft or strong
But moo a merry song
Moo a merry song. Moo a merry song
As you move a long, long, long
Moo a merry song, moo a merry song
As you move a long

Hounslow Mayor Sham Jessar and his wife launch the Centre Space panto.

He's behind you!

HOUNSLOW'S Mayor and Mayoress were horsing around in the Treaty Centre to help launch this year's Centre Space pantomime.

A pantomime horse presented our number one citizens with cash and goodies raised and donated during a stunt raid on local shops by the star of the show, Robin Hood.

The Mayor's charities will benefit from the stunt.

Robin Hood and Babes in the Wood is the panto at Centre Space and it runs from Thursday, December 27 to Saturday, January 12. Tickets are available from the box office on 081-577 6968.

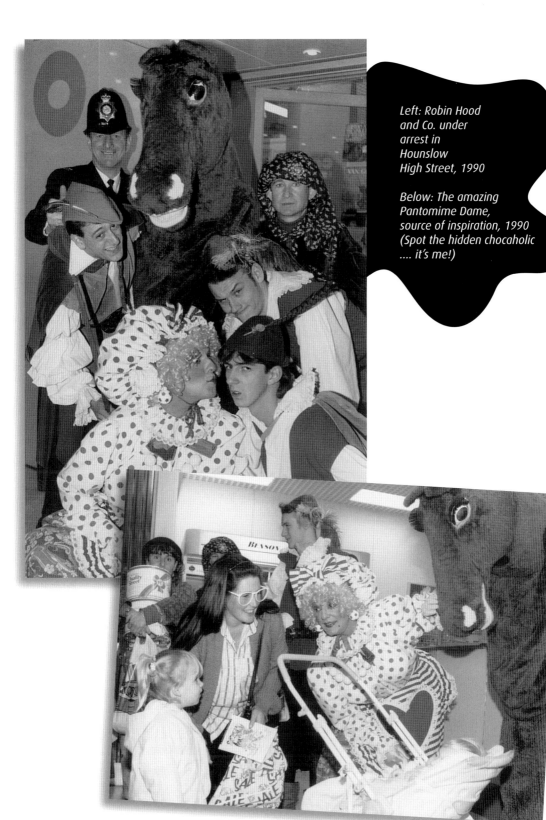

Left: Robin Hood
and Co. under
arrest in
Hounslow
High Street, 1990

Below: The amazing
Pantomime Dame,
source of inspiration, 1990
(Spot the hidden chocaholic
.... it's me!)

Dick Whittington returns from the Far East, 1989

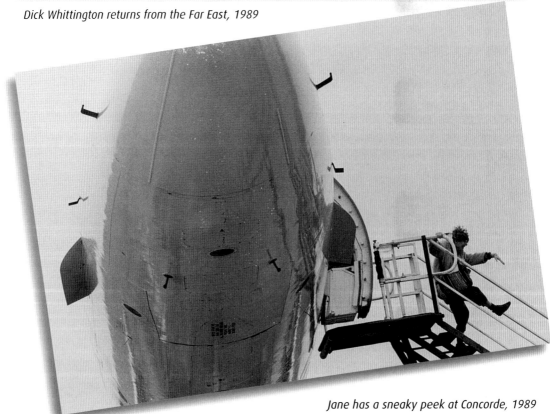

Jane has a sneaky peek at Concorde, 1989

ADULT FANCY DRESS COSTUMES

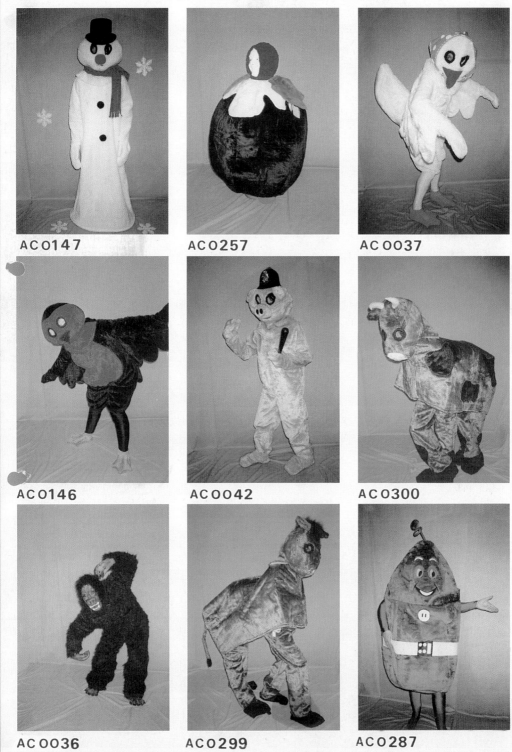

ACO147

ACO257

ACOO37

ACO146

ACOO42

ACO300

ACOO36

ACO299

ACO287

Gay Time and Gala – Costume wish list, 1990

Supercow Climbs Mount Everest

Woke up this morning feeling very depressed... but not to worry because I am SUPERCOW, I can do anything. One squeeze of my marigold udder and I am transformed.

A quick moo and I'm off, flying out of the window, above the Friesian clouds to Nepal and the foot of the Himalayas. Supercow has no fear. Supercow is the bravest cow in the West, now in the East.

I skip up the mountain with ease, passing tourists, trekkers and sherpas as I go. I am Supercow, the famous mountain climber. People laugh, stare and wave. They all love Supercow. In my magic Supercow pocket I have concealed a special Friesian flag.... I have reached the summit. I am not out of breath. I sing a very powerful and beautiful summit-reaching song as I plant my Friesian flag on the foot of Mount Everest.

I now reveal my unbelievable inflatable paraglider, which has been hiding in my left secret pocket. I give it a shake, pop it on with elegance and ease and glide down the mountain with distant cheers of all my adoring fans ringing in my ears as I make my graceful descent.

Naughty Grand Old Duke Song

Adapted from traditional nursery rhyme
- collected by Jonah and Toby, with extra 'cow bit' by their mum.

O the grand Old Duke of York, he had ten thousand men, he
marched them up to the top of the hill and he marched them
down again,
And when they were up they were up, and when they were down
they were down, And when they were only half way up, their
trousers all fell down.

O fantastic Supercow, she can defy all men,
She's marched right up to the top of the hill
And she'll float back down again
And now she is right at the top,
And soon she will have to come down
With a squeeze of an udder
And a moo and a shudder
She's the bravest cow in town

Travels in the United Kingdom

Most of my moovements in and around the United Kingdom have been confined to the South, but this was not for want of trying. Maybe because I was born a Southerner the higher forces weren't keen to let my cows and me go past Milton Keynes. Well that's my excuse anyway. Worms and I did pay a brief visit to Edinburgh one Hogmanay but I don't think she ever came out of her compression pack, it was a bit too noisy and scary, and I was a bit too sober. Of course New Year's Eve in Amsterdam was quite a different story, but I'll tell you about that later.

My first major trip out and about with Worms (yuck) was an evening in London, and I still have clear memories of that exciting expedition. Jamie, a work colleague, soon to be on sick leave with chronic backache, came along. I also persuaded my 'boatmate' Mike to join us. Luckily he was a professional photographer! Jamie transpired to be a very loyal back end to my cow and this was his first experience of the joys of bending over continually for more than an hour on the trot (only one pun intended, and not the rude one).

The photographs are self explanatory, though I have omitted the rather rude one of a man relating to the back end of the cow. This is a family book after all. Several men tried to relate to Worms' back end in this rather unfortunate manner; no further explanation needed. A really friendly doorman at The Ritz related to Worms' front end in a very kindly manner and let us go in to use the loos without a merest pull on the tail, though he did ask us to remove the costume first.

This first London visit was one of many forays up to Town. In 1993/94 Jamie and I became very enthusiastic about busking and would spend many a merry weekend in Leicester Square entertaining bemused onlookers, or was it onlooker. Anyway, at least we enjoyed ourselves. We had a specially customised tape for our little busking set including songs such as Teddy Bears' Picnic, Remember You're a Womble and The Muppet Theme Song. While the rather knackered ghetto blaster blasted out jolly tunes Jamie and I would leap around 'incogcowho, incownito', attempting to be entertaining. Puppets would spontaneously appear from the cow's nether regions, on cue, with appropriate lyrics in the songs. Teddy bears would frequently get lost in the frenzied scramble to change busking location. Please use your imagination. We used a very creepy looking ventriloquist's doll belonging to Jamie called Mr Chips, who eerily squeaked the Muppet theme song. Come to think of it, he reminds me of a character in a horror film I once saw. I don't know what our little show looked like, as I was rather too busy being inside the cow making sure none of my bodily parts were showing (7 years' bad luck if you expose a body part, clothed or unclothed, from inside a pantomime cow). I'm sure we heard the occasional titter or embarrassed laugh but unless my ears were deceiving me, we never drew a crowd, or even a mini crowd. I remember I really enjoyed the chaotic logistics of trying to turn on the tape recorder and then quickly getting back into the cow whilst retaining anonymity. It was most probably that superhero feeling again.

Unfortunately we have no photographic record of our busking endeavours as Mike sensibly avoided these little outings. In fact his life literally would have been in danger, as we soon discovered.

Our busking career came to a sudden shocking end when were told by a very cross member of the busking community that we were busking on his patch. I will spare you the details of exactly what he said and the manner in which it was conveyed, but it was very scary. Honest. We did try to reason with him, and explain we didn't realise it was so territorial but, as you can imagine, he didn't take too kindly to this either. We would not be deterred and had a brief moment of glory busking in Covent Garden, where within 5 minutes we were moved on by the police for not having a special Covent Garden Busking Licence. At this point we decided to retire from busking and re-launch ourselves as entertainers at children's birthday parties.

Our first engagement as kids' entertainers was, I am ashamed to say, also our last; I did have another try at it 5 years later, but on my own. Jamie and I were asked to provide entertainment for a 3 year old's party, a friend of a work colleague's young daughter. Just the sight of the rather unruly pantomime cow sent the entire group of about twenty 3 year olds into complete hysterics, and they were definitely not happy hysterics. We carried on relentless, presuming that our wonderful kiddy-friendly songs and puppets would cheer them up, but the sight of Mr Chips and the collection of flying teddies only increased the hysteria, and eventually a rather distraught parent stuck her head sunnyside up and politely told us to stop. It was all rather embarrassing and after scoffing lots of party food, including pink biscuits (yum, yum, my favourite) we refused the money and scarpered, tail between Jamie's legs. After a few similar experiences with under 4's I have now learned that, with or without a terrible show on top, pantomime creatures are generally very bad news for this age group, who still cannot distinguish between fantasy and reality. Glen, an old college friend, has never forgiven me for the terrible nightmares his then 3 year old son experienced after Worms made one of her spontaneous appearances at a Festival Ceildh. Incidentally, I have discovered that the under 2's are generally o.k. with pantomime creatures. I presume this is because to them everything and everybody looks fairly peculiar anyway.

In the last few years, leaving a short gap for recovery from the first party experience, Worms and Snailey have appeared at parties, both as entertainers and as guests. Snailey joined us in 1996, as I will soon explain. When my friends started getting married it seemed only fitting that two romancing cows should take the floor for the second dance (not the first I hasten to add). My kids usually have a cow bringing in the birthday cake at their parties. In fact only a few weeks ago I had a rather interesting experience at Toby's party. We were all set to bring on the cake with cow in tow when I realised I didn't have a back end, Dan, my husband, being tied up with duties such as cake-lighting and child control. The assembled parents looked aghast when I tried to persuade them of the benefits of the role, both in terms of fitness and the doing of a kind and generous act. They all refused apart from one slightly terrified-looking mum whom I eventually managed to persuade. I noticed she was literally shaking when putting the costume on and had a very unhappy expression on her face. When I gave her an opt out clause, she grabbed it.

Eventually I had to nab a member of staff at the Leisure Centre, where the party was held, and virtually stuff her into the cow suit. After all, I explained, they were paid to help us provide the party. It was rather a traumatic experience for everyone involved, but it was worth it in the end. At least it inspired my song 'I wandered lonely as a cow', which I am particularly pleased with. Incidentally, at this particular party one four year old girl whose family are dairy farmers was very upset by the cow. Though I was obviously sorry about this I was impressed that even at a ripe old age Worms still has some resemblance of cow in her, even to those in the know.

Back down memory lane again... Shortly after Worms' first trip to London in 1991, Jamie, Mike and I decide to take her to Windsor Castle for a quick mingle with royalty. These are some of my favourite pictures as the waxwork models are so incredibly life-like and Worms' looks very important. It was quite tricky trying to sneak under the barriers to get the pictures taken without the museum curators spotting us. I'm sure The Queen would forgive us, as hopefully a few of her subjects, or whatever you call them, will have a bit of a giggle at the pictures. Security around the castle grounds was obviously much tighter. A policeman immediately approached us during our trot around the gardens. He was very polite, and though we had to 'decow' we were able to continue to wander at our leisure.

Jamie and I were wild and free in those early twenty-something days! We would go nightclubbing at least twice a week and would take the cow to 'The Fridge' in Brixton, and to 'Heaven on The Embankment'. I remember going up on the stage once at The Fridge, in between one of their incredibly trendy, sexy live shows. Of course we were the trendiest, sexiest thing that anyone had ever seen. It was another moment of shining glory. On a rather less glorious note Jamie and I got 'cowed up' and paid a weekly visit to the staff canteen at Hounslow Council's Civic Centre. We use to amble past the happy munchers mooing as we went. It certainly livened up a dull lunchtime and it was always fun to hear the banter back at the office, with members of staff speculating about who were the wearers of the mysterious cow. (It's that super hero fetish again.)

Though I have had my slightly rebellious cow-like moments, Worms can also do good deeds. In the early 90's she always attended the Swimathon with me, some confused spectator being grabbed for a rear-end position.

She also tried to encourage the couch potatoes off their sofas by promoting the importance of exercise for a local leisure centre in Richmond. This was during my addiction to Step Aerobics. My Occupational Therapy training had its jolly moments when I took Worms and Snailey along to various health care settings to provide a bit of laughter-therapy to patients and staff, and definitely to myself!!

I had a strong instinct that Worms was destined for altruistic pursuits. With this in mind in 1993, when Worms and I were still going through our honeymoon period, we decided to hitch to John O'Groats dressed as a pantomime cow, hoping to raise funds for Red Nose Day. Jamie agreed to be my back end and we thought it would probably take us about 24 hours. This made allowance for a night's sleep that some kind hotel owner was bound to provide for us. This was one of Jamie's last ventures as back end of cow, as it was shortly after this that he developed chronic backache. A five-hour Gay Rights Samba Parade later on that year was the straw that broke the cow's back... not literally, I'm relieved to say.

Mike made us a wonderful sign, which we attached to the body of the cow. It read 'Give us a lift for Red Nose Day'. The cow wore a striking red nose and her first freshly-made pair of udders. I was able to secure some form of sponsorship from a courier company who guaranteed to pick us up if we got stranded in a remote village. This was, of course, providing we were able to ring them for a lift. They also dropped us off at a suitable starting point on the M4. We got an amazing £650 sponsorship from friends and colleagues and we also hoped to rattle a tin along the way. A bit awkward in a cow suit, but we managed. It was a very slow business, not helped at all by torrential rain. We just took any lifts we could get going anywhere, but it seemed to take forever. I expect no one was keen to have a sopping wet cow in his or her car. I only remember two lifts very clearly, probably because there weren't many of them. One was from an ageing hippy in a Volkswagen van who thought the whole thing was very funny and happily stuffed a note into our collection box, and the final lift was from a Rentokil rep who was visiting Blenheim Palace. After having soaked his car with soggy cow, we couldn't bring ourselves to dangle the collection box in his face. We were thoroughly fed up at this point, and Jamie's back was really starting to suffer so we rang DHL, the couriers, and persuaded them to come and rescue us. I did manage to find some confused passers-by to take a couple of photos of the cow in villages along the way, but unfortunately after our return, my car was broken into and the camera was stolen. Still at least we hadn't asked people to sponsor us per mile!! And we did make lots of money even if it hadn't all been a bundle of laughs.

In 1995 I decided to cast off my charitable udders and became enraptured by the idea of fame and fortune. After seeing an advertisement in 'The Stage' I applied for an audition to be the pantomime cow on a big billboard advertising British Airways in Hong Kong. I was told that David Bailey would be taking the pictures so I knew it had to be important. I got together cow curriculum vitae and then convinced myself the job was for me. Jamie was, by now, living in Hong Kong so it seemed that fate was in my backside, if you see what I mean. It seemed natural that they would send me off to Hong Kong to rendezvous with my original back end and then our life of fame and fortune would begin.

The audition was really very funny, with cows of many shapes and sizes waiting for their pictures to be taken. It was screamingly obvious, even at this early stage, that despite winning hands down for compact ability, Worms wasn't exactly a looker. There were cows with flashing eyelids and moving jaws, cows with long wiggling horns, and even one with flashing nostrils; then Worms with his rather squishy face from spending too many hours in a compression pack. Still, I held a glimmer of hope. After all my back end did live in Hong Kong.

I waited expectantly for the phone to ring and after two agonising weeks, fantasising about my first class ticket to Hong Kong, I rang the advertising agency. It was not to be! The job had gone to a husband and wife team, with flashing eyelids, squeaking udders and a swishing tail. I decided Worms and I had a purer destiny. We were too good for petty, materialistic advertising campaigns; though it was rather upsetting when we visited Hong Kong two years later, to see another cow on a huge flashing British Airways billboard with its name up in lights.

In 1996 Snailey was born. He was meant to be a Hereford bull copy of Worms and is, in a manner of speaking. I think the kindly dressmaker from Hounslow went a bit wrong in the making, as he definitely doesn't fit properly, especially at the back end. He also has a very pink snout, not that that is necessarily a bad thing. However, as previously mentioned, he has been very useful and mostly user friendly at the various weddings I've attended in the last few years, including my own. It seemed only natural to upgrade from one cow to two once my friends started getting hitched. It gives attending weddings more of a sense of purpose. Or perhaps it's the Jewish Matchmaker in me coming out in a rather unusual fashion. He definitely has a strong male energy and rarely wears his satin udders.

Our first expedition with Snailey was to Milton Keynes to meet the famous concrete cows. For some unknown reason I decided to leave Worms behind. I think I wanted to give my new cow some special attention. It was also the first cow outing I had made with my future husband, Dan. There was something rather romantic about the outing. There I was in the middle of a concrete jungle with my new cow and my new man. This may be the only time anyone has thought of Milton Keynes being remotely romantic. Anyway the experience obviously didn't put Dan off, and we took some very mooving pictures of Snailey cavorting with the concrete cows.

And the thrills and spills of Milton Keynes wasn't the only exciting place I went with my furry friend...

Above:
Kindly Doorman at The Ritz, 1991

Left: Strange men politely stroking the cow's back end, 1991

Opposite page:

Top: On Westminster Bridge, 1991
Middle: Trooping of the colour in Windsor Castle, 1991
Bottom: Outside Windsor Castle, 1991

This page:

Above:
Nicola's 5th
birthday party,
1992

Left: Dan and
Worms presenting
the cake at Toby's
5th birthday party,
2005

Top: Romance on Richmond
Tow Path, 1996

Below: Cornwall, 1992

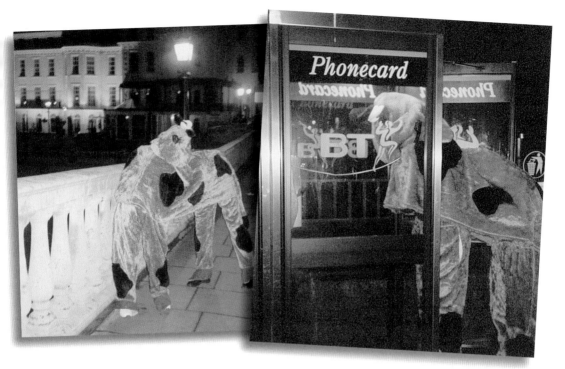

Above left: Richmond Bridge, 1996 Right: Quick call, 1996   Below: Milton Keynes, 1996

ROTATE
ME TO
VIEW

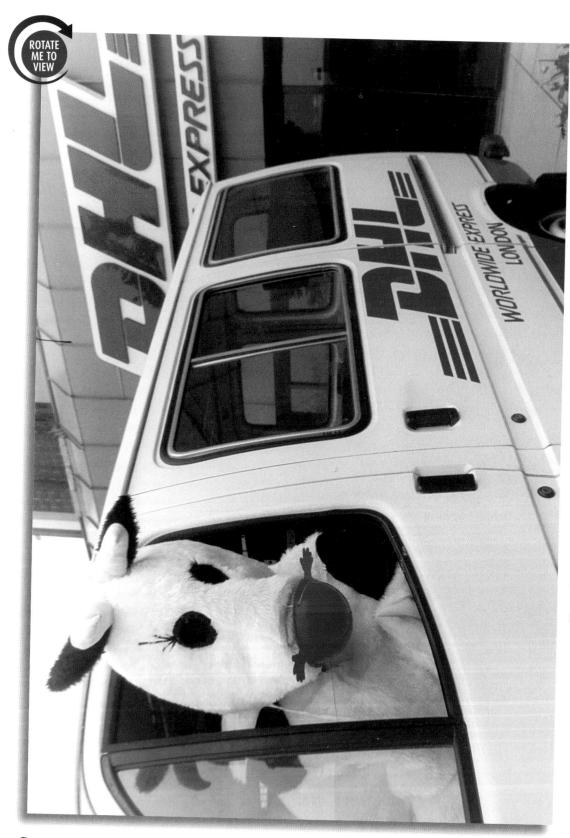

Top: Nelson Hospital, 1997

Right: Royal Hospital for Neurodisability, 1998

Opposite page: Red Nose Cow, 1991

Opposite page:

Top: Steph and Mel's wedding, 1995

Below left: Jane's 30th birthday party in a Greek restaurant

Below right: Swimathon, 1993

This page:

Top: Step Aerobics 1994

Above: "I thought Occupational Therapists made baskets not dragons!" OT Training 1997

Supercow Prima Ballerina

...and Ice Skater extraordinaire!

Felt a bit queasy on waking, too much late night bingeing, nothing that a bit of fresh air wouldn't cure. O to feel the wind in my........ udders! Yes, it's me again – SUPERCOW. I'm up like a bolt of lightening, leaping over the moon (the sun isn't up yet) and off to Kew gardens. When I arrive, the crowds have already gathered, lining my path and I parade down the leafy boulevard towards the beautiful outdoor ice rink. It's a glorious sunny day and I am wearing my petite pink tutu. I am as graceful as a butterfly, as I arabesque (technical dancey word) towards my destination. I can see my old ballet teacher, Mrs Crossface, amongst the multitudes and she is showering me with love, pride and kisses. She was my inspiration for dance. I am covered with rose petals thrown by my adoring fans and cushioning my hoofey steps as my udders sway gracefully in the breeze.

As I arrive at the Island of Glass (hum, I am definitely trying a bit too hard to be writerish) I am serenaded by a string quartet playing graceful ice-skatey-type music. Miraculously, beautiful white skates suddenly appear on my hooves and I'm off, gliding on the surface of the rink, a picture of femininity serenity and beauty. I am Sibblis (something like that), goddess of beauty.

I dance the night away, still pirouetting as the sun rises. All the crowds have gone home, but I linger on, a beautiful silhouette under the light of the Silvery Moon.

Old Oak Tree anon.
Collected from children's singing group

Under the Shade of the old oak tree
I see the moon and the moon sees me
Please let the light that shines on me
Shine on the ones I love
Over the mountains over the seas
Back where my heart is longing to be
Please let the light that shines on me
Shine on the ones I love

Mulberry Moon
Extract from a poem by Edward Lear,
'The Quangle Wangle's Hat', with tune by Juliet Harwood

And at night by the light of the Mulberry moon
They danced to the flute of the Blue Baboon
On the broad green leaves of the Crumpetty Tree
And all were as happy
As happy could be
With the Quangle Wangle Quee

Travels in Europe

Worms' first trot overseas was a skiing holiday in Flaine, France in 1992. For most of the time it was less of a trot and more of a splat, and I'm pleased to say that I was an observer for a change. Luckily there were a number of confident skiers in our group as there is no way you'd catch me skiing down a very steep mountain in a cow suit. It was my second time skiing and balance is definitely not one of my strong points.

What I found most fascinating about the skiing cow side of the experience was that in this large French resort, with mostly French people on the slopes, no one took much notice, or seemed that surprised to see a pantomime cow zooming down the hill. In fact I found the lack of reaction much more interesting than the skiing cow itself. All I can assume is that these particular French people have a very different sense of humour from our own, or maybe don't have a sense of humour (no offence intended dear French person, I am just weighing up the options). Maybe the French often go skiing dressed as pantomime creatures. Maybe they presumed it was a real cow enjoying a day out and thought it impolite to stare. Who knows? I found it all very fascinating. I was so busy psychoanalysing the French one sunny skiing afternoon that I got completely lost on one of these multi-resort adventures you can go on in the Alps and eventually I fell off a ski lift and had to be rescued by a 'skiing motorbike-type thingy'. Mr Skiing motorbike was very handsome and it was all rather exciting, though, disappointingly, none of our group had noticed my absence, or really seemed to care about my exciting adventure. Thank goodness I'd had the cow suit with me during that holiday. It gave me something to talk to, even if it was a furry creature, unstuffed.

The same year I went with my boyfriend at the time, soon to be my ex, and my cow, to Amsterdam. There may well have been a link between our relationship's rapid demise and the cow's increasing importance, who knows, it was never discussed in depth, I expect he felt too silly to mention it. The boyfriend of course, not the cow.

The experience I had as a cow in Amsterdam was very similar to that in France, in that nobody really seemed to notice or to care. I must add at this point that the boyfriend was in the cow with me so it was quite difficult to gauge people's reactions. My experience so far was that people who noticed usually made a noise, and very little noise was made directly at us. I suspect their reasons for apparent inertia, or should I say disinterest, were quite different from the French reasons. Of course I never tried it myself but I have been told that cannabis, which I believe is widely available in Amsterdam, can cause you to be rather apathetic, and immune to reacting to wandering cows. The other possible reason was that we misheard the loud reaction because we had eaten too much space flavoured chocolate cake, or because of the loud bangers firing away to bring in the New Year. Whatever the reason, it became increasingly pleasant to be inside a nice cosy cow when it was loud and cold outside.

Worms' last trip to Europe was in 1993 when I took him to the Hungarian plains to save the Great Bustard (no, I don't mean the newly ex-boyfriend). We went as a part of a conservation holiday run by the British Trust of Conservation Volunteers. I decided to take Worms because I'd just dyed my hair a scary maroon colour and I needed something to hide in. I was also recovering from the end of a long relationship so it was good to have a special friend with me, even if he did spend most of the holiday inside a compression pack It was a very busy couple of weeks and not much of a holiday at all. We spent a lot of time rustling around in bushes looking for Great Bustards and turning the Bustards eggs at 3 am in the morning. To clarify, the unhatched eggs were kept in incubators in the conservation centre where we were staying. Every three hours these eggs needed to be turned and it was the volunteers' job to do the turning at ridiculous times of night. A bit like breast-feeding but without the milk or breast. Of course I did have a breast at that time, and an udder too, but they weren't needed on this particular occasion.

I did manage to spot a couple of Great Bustards during the trip but quite frankly I preferred the storks, who just nested quietly on top of telegraph poles and didn't make any demands on you in the middle of the night.

There was hardly anytime to lark around dressed as a cow, and the conservation bit was all rather serious so I tried to put all thoughts of sneaking up on Great Bustards in cow costume out of my mind, though I suspect it would have been very funny. On the last night of the project we had a special meal so Worms came out at a Hungarian restaurant! The locals really loved her and I did regret not having given her more of an airing. The next day I took her for a wander around the local village and she caused much hilarity. The back end in this instance was an 18-year old student, Lucy, who was part of the conservation group from the U.K. After her role as back end we became good friends and stayed in contact for several years. She ended up working in conservation and the last time I heard from her she was saving elephants in Kenya.

Though Worms did not venture far into Europe her little visits were varied and gave a few of us some happy memories. In addition I have learnt the valuable, life-changing lesson that skiing trips and visits to Amsterdam are definitely more exciting if you happen to have a spare pantomime cow, or two. The experience is likely to be even better if you allow time to sample the local chocolate cake!

Skiing in Flaine, 1992 (continued overleaf)

This page:

Above: Skiing in Flaine, 1992
Left: Turning the Bustards eggs! 1993
Below: On the Hungarian Plains, 1993

Opposite page:

Top left: Lucy with Hungarian cherries, 1993
Top right: Shopping in Hungary, 1993
Bottom: Scenic Hungarian village, 1993

Supercow Chef Extraordinaire

A rather groggy feeling on waking, but not for long cos in the flick of an udder (ouch) I'm off – a cow with a mission. I am the world famous Cordonbleaueeux chef SUPERCOW. Today I am a very special and extremely mysterious guest at a top London restaurant, the ever so trendy Nicefoodtaste.com. I arrive in my specially designed Phillippe Gaudi top-chef-cow-cook-wear, ready to rustle up one of my incredible culinary creations in front of a live audience. Renowned for my brilliance, chefs who are 'in the know' come from miles around to watch my special techniques. In less than two minutes I have rustled up the most miraculous, mouth watering choo choo pastry with a soufflée filling, and knobs on top. On the side I have created a delicate, lightly-dressed salad with hand crafted tomatoes and radishes in the shape of miniature peaked udders. Am I not cow extraordinaire?? Are there no limits to my talents ?

Three lucky prizewinners, from an incredibly important competition get to taste the merest morsel of the fruits of my labour. All are stunned. How can a living being create such delights. The flabbergasted onlookers head home.....as I quickly scoff the rest of the grub and run like the wind back to my abode, where I produce tasteful home made dinners and nutritious, creative packed lunches for my little calvelets. Without a doubt I am the envy of all the cow mothers in town.

How does a Brown Cow give White Milk

Collected by Cathie Hodgson

How does a brown cow give white milk when he only eats
green grass?
How does a brown cow give white milk when he only eats
green grass?
What is your suggestion to this simple question?
You don't know, I don't know, You only have to ask
How does a brown cow give white milk when he only eats
green grass?

Why has the Cow got Four Legs?

Collected by Charlie the parrot

Why has the cow got four legs?
I must find out somehow
You don't know and I don't know and
Neither does the cow !

Travels in The Americas

'Wordly-wise Cow'
Designed by Steve Cribb, 1992

Our expeditions to the American Continent were extremely varied. Worms accompanied me for the first section of my journey through South America, which were some of my most exciting travels.

Before leaving home I became very enthusiastic about the idea of the British Council sponsoring me to travel around with Worms and teach locals the history of British pantomime. I became so enraptured by my brilliant scheme that I spent most of my spare time at The British Theatre Museum in Covent Garden doing my research. The theatre I was working in was promoting a few performances from overseas supported by Visiting Arts' grants provided through The British Council. I was sure that there must be heaps of money for me to fund my amazing 'one cow' show, with the added benefit of my British Pantomime Educational Pack. I'm sure, dear reader, you will be really disappointed to know that I have misplaced all my valuable research so I will not be able to share it with you. There will be no extended history lesson on The Early Pantomime Cow, but I do recall that it was something to do with late nineteenth century music hall. After several "O yes you will, O no you won't" type telephone conversations with various people from The British Council there was a definite 'O no you won't' letter. So unsurprisingly I didn't get an all expenses paid trip around South America, courtesy of The British Council, but at least I tried. They didn't even give me a new pair of marigold gloves to replace my cow's rather tatty udders (shame, boo hiss etc).

Not deterred by their lack of interest, I gallantly produced 20 British Pantomime Information Packs, which I carefully secreted in my ever-expanding backpack. My travelling companion was becoming increasing fraught about the quantity of necessities in his pack in comparison to the ever increasing array of interesting items in mine.

Before we left the U.K I had a party in my flat in Richmond. My landlord was away, so it seemed like a good opportunity to have a little farewell bash. I hired a badge machine especially for the event and all the guests were obliged to make at least one badge in a cow design. More than a hundred badges were made, and there probably would have been more if my landlord hadn't decided to come back a day early from his trip away.

Steve, a good friend of mine was not able to come to the party. He used a wheelchair and it was impossible to get a wheelchair up the flat's old rickety stairs. Instead he sent me a design, that I turned into a badge and also superimposed on all the writing paper I used on my travels. Steve was a brilliant artist and because he had no use of his hands, he did his drawing on the computer using his mouth and limited head movements. As well as being a great design, this particular drawing is important to me as Steve died shortly after my return from South America (see page 47).

We arrived in Santiago, Chile in November 1992. Besides a large compression pack containing the cow attached to my backpack, I had 100 cow badges, and of course 20 secret documents. This first month travelling with my boyfriend was rather tense. As well as his personal luggage he was carrying our sleeping bags, cooker, tent, and First Aid kit. I was carrying all my essential cow related items, and my own clothes!

Apart from my very cumbersome backpack and the tension between Daniel and me, my main memories of the first month of this trip were the amazing volcanoes and two very jolly Canadian women that we travelled with. I would like to explain at this point that Daniel was my soon-to-be ex where as Dan, who will also appear on occasions is my later-to-be husband. I did think of all sorts of other jolly names to avoid any confusion but I think I was probably the only one who thought they were appropriate, or dare I say it....funny. With the help of the two Canadians we took some wonderful pictures of the cow. We visited a seaside resort, La Serena, where Worms had a terrifying close encounter with a lama, and then we went on to visit a fantastic moon-like landscape in a region of central Chile. This area was close to San Pedro, where you can meet the oldest woman in the world who is mummified in sand. She dates back to 8000BC. From here we decided to go on an 'organised' tour into The Atacama Desert.

We were then going to head up more than 14,000 feet above sea level to visit the Geysers de Tatio, and stay in a visitors' centre near by. We were told that if we were at all susceptible to altitude sickness, this is where we were likely to get it, but there wasn't much that could be done to alleviate it. A few of us tried chewing a leaf called coca, which is pretty disgusting, but is meant to help. The locals are addicted to this leaf. Not surprising really, as it is the original source of cocaine.

The area in which we were staying was one of the most beautiful I have ever seen. We were completely surrounded by live volcanoes. It looked even more dramatic at this time because it had been snowing, which apparently was very unusual. We headed through the desert and up the mountain in a large 4x4 jeep. There were 8 of us, a real mixed bunch including a doctor, a superman type character who had travelled extensively, the two Canadian women, a very funny Finnish couple and Daniel and me. The driver spoke broken English so we could just about make out what he was saying however he certainly very clear about being paid in advance.

After a 3-hour drive we made it to the top of the mountain. The geysers were a terrific place for a 'cow pose' and we got some fantastic pictures of the cow surrounded by smoke and hot springs. The doctor had a really bad time with altitude sickness but the rest of us were symptom free. Because the snow was getting heavier the driver decided that we should leave early afternoon and try to get back before darkness and the big freeze.

Our journey back was hellish from beginning to end. Because of the heavy snow fall, the driver was confused and couldn't identify his usual landmarks. We got completely lost and then to put the icing on the cake, or the snow in our case, the jeep ran out of fuel. How he could have been silly enough to let this happen I don't know. Obviously we were rather stuck as, unsurprisingly there are no petrol stations in the middle of The Atacama desert, and no MacDonald's either! The driver was in a complete panic and started crying, which wasn't very reassuring. He then headed off into the snowy desert looking for help. To be honest I wasn't sure that this was the most sensible strategy, but there was no reasoning with him. This was also before the days of a zillion mobile phones so we weren't able to get help this way either. The Superman person also decided to wander off into the desert in the opposite direction. Neither of them were dressed for snowy conditions so we tried to persuade them not to go, but they went and we were left to gently freeze together. Fortunately we did have a couple of sleeping bags with us, but most importantly we had three large parts of warm furry cow costume, which were literally a lifesaver. This was definitely Worms' most heroic moment to date. We were all in rather a panic, and the doctor was no use at all because she was still recovering from altitude sickness. As night fell we just snuggled together in sleeping bags and cow and shared out the couple of cereal bars we had between us. I know it all sounds rather dramatic, but to be honest, it was. I seriously thought that we'd had our chips. I probably won the prize for the most panic stricken person and the Finns for the funniest persons. Everyone else was quite calm, considering. The doctor was too busy still feeling sick to show any emotion at all.

Amazingly at the break of day help came. Superman had found another jeep wandering around and managed to get us fuel. The jeep then found our very freezing driver, who was now warmly back in the village. Another chap drove us all back to La Serena. We were all so relieved to be rescued that we didn't bother getting angry with the tour organisers, and as far as I know no one even asked for a refund! Though it had been a very frightening experience I was thrilled that it was Worms, closely followed by Superman, who had saved the day.

On the next leg of our journey we travelled overland from Chile to Bolivia. Arriving in La Paz on a rickety old bus felt unreal, almost like descending into a huge bowl on the top of the world. Initially the high altitude was hard to cope with, especially as there was a lot of uphill walking in order to get anywhere. We timed our arrival to coincide with The Gran Poder, a huge festival in la Paz, the main event being an enormous carnival parade through the streets.

The evening before the great festival was an event in itself. Families began transferring their entire living rooms into the streets. Armchairs, sofas and tables strategically lined the streets as people clamoured to save the best viewing positions. The following evening the carnival began, and by now the tables lining the pavements were covered in edible goodies, some for sale but mostly for the families themselves. The floats themselves were spectacular, most accompanied by dancers and brass bands. The music was very jazzy, with a Latin beat obviously! The whole of Bolivia seemed to arrive in La Paz for this event. The clothes worn by the local people were in beautiful bright colours, and the spectators looked just as good as the performers. It was predominantly the women who wore the traditional costumes.

Worms then had her little moment of glory. We paraded up and down our little section of street, handing out cow badges to the children that we met. This was quite some feat from inside a pantomime cow but we managed. We were excused from our 'seven years bad luck for showing bodily parts' on this particular occasion. You will have to imagine this merry scene as I have no photographic evidence to prove it. For some reason we didn't take pictures of the event. Perhaps because it was enough hassle just trying to stay in costume and hand out badges amongst the huge crowds. At this point we had parted company with our Canadian friends and didn't have other travelling companions to take pictures, or be back ends, for us.

Next we headed to Peru for the last lap of Worms' travels with us, the weight of the extra cow becoming more cumbersome as we acquired more and more souvenirs. The main reason we'd brought Worms was for La Gran Poder so if the opportunity arose, now would have been an ideal time to say our goodbyes. I was tempted to take her on to Cuzco for a huge festival called Inti Raymi, and then on to Machu Picchu, but sensibly Daniel thought this wasn't a great idea as both Machu Picchu and Inti Raymi have sacred significance, and Worms' isn't exactly sacred. After attending Inti Raymi I realised the sacred parts were partially submerged in a sea of alcohol, and I doubt whether Worms would have caused any concern.

A couple of years later I heard that there was a big 'Travellers' Full Moon Party' at Machu Picchu. During such a party Worms might have been quite happy at this sacred sight, but after visiting the amazing place itself I was pleased to have been cowless. This was partly because of the sacredness of the place, and partly because of the eight hour journey on foot from Cuzco to Matchu Picchu. I found the walking incredibly hard and definitely appreciated a lighter backpack.

Fate was looking after me as on our train journey to Cuzco we met a guardian angel disguised as a young man called Ivon. He was travelling loosely homeward having attended the Ecological Summit in Rio, Brazil. As a journalist working for the United Nations he was looking for adventure, and had decided to hitch-hike through Bolivia to Chile to catch his plane home from Santiago. He was hoping to travel all the way by truck! He seemed positively delighted at the prospect of taking the cow with him, and we hastily swapped addresses and arranged to meet up on our return to the U.K. I handed over the compression pack with a fair amount of trepidation, but several months later Worms was safely returned. Apparently they had travelled by truck to Chile, and throughout the entire journey Worms had remained safely compressed.

Worms also came to North America with me in 1995 when Mum and I went to a family reunion in Chicago. This huge event involved a lot of eating, and meeting people that you had nothing in common with and would probably never meet again. Much to my mother's displeasure I insisted on taking the cow. As there were only 4 British representatives at the reunion I thought it would be a good idea to take a bit of extra British culture with us. Worms came out once at the huge banquet event, and I managed to persuade a distant cousin a millions times removed to be the back-end. Mum took a few dodgy pictures as a memento. Worms' visit didn't end on a very smiley note. I hadn't taken the compression pack with me on this occasion, as it was more of a posh suitcase kind of holiday. Well, it was posh suitcase until I managed to break it just before our homeward journey. It was literally bursting at the seams with cow and udders and then sort of erupted all over our posh hotel room. As you can imagine Mum wasn't too impressed, and it does seem to be her resounding memory of that holiday - The Incredible Exploding Cow Adventure.

Left: Cow and lama in La Serena, Chile, 1992

Opposite page: Geysers de Tatio, 1992

Canadians and Cow in the Atacama Desert, 1992

Upside down Desert Cow, 1992

Right side up Desert Cow, 1992

Family re-union in Chicago, 1995

Supercow juggles down the Thames

Woke up feeling a bit jittery. Check the calendar. Could it be pre-menstrual cow syndrome? Resist the urge to gobble down half a ton of chocolate. In a chew of the cud (muesli) I am transformed. Yes, you've guessed it. It's me, SUPERCOW, ready to productively and ever so sensibly transform my jitteriness into purposeful activity.

I water ski down the Thames to 'Circus Space', the heart of all circus activity in London. I perform the occasional twirly whirl as I go. I am drawn by my private boat steered by my spouse, who unfortunately has no sense of direction, so whilst skiing I am also map reading, shouting directions to him from the back of the boat.

I am the star of Circus Space and when we arrive my equipment is waiting for me in my own private dressing room. Up onto the tight rope I leap, 8 juggling clubs in hooves. With a dash of meths and a flick from my lighter they are aflame. My performance is captivating (even if I say so myself). Many oo's and aah's from the audience as I handle the clubs with such skill. Onlookers are so enthralled that they burst into a spontaneous samba routine using everything and anything as percussion. I juggle to the rhythm of their playing. The atmosphere is electric. I am so high on the rapturous applause that I levitate and find myself juggling in mid air. I manage to fasten myself back onto my water skis and zoom back home along the Thames, with on-looking boats all honking their horns and cheering as I pass.

O What a Funny Farm
By Chris Blanchard

Down on the farm I saw a cow, saw a cow it was
  going bow wow,
Saw a cow it was going bow wow
O what a funny farm

Down on the farm I saw a dog
Saw a dog with its face in a bog
Saw a dog with his face in a bog
O what a funny farm

Down at the farm I saw a duck
Saw a duck that was going cluck, cluck,
Saw a duck that was going cluck, cluck
O what a funny farm.

(Chris encourages singers to add their own made up verses.)

Travels in Asia

In 1996 Worms came with me to Thailand where we attended a twenty-day silent meditation retreat at a Buddhist monastery, Wat Kow Tham, on the island of Koh Pahngan. It was my second retreat at this particular monastery, and especially challenging as it was the longest amount of time I have ever had to remain silent. I had just about managed 10 days last time. As with other things in my life, I'm not quite sure why I wanted to do it, but it seemed like a good idea at the time!

Dan and I had travelled to India earlier on in the year but decided not to take Worms as we were worried about offending the locals – the cow being a holy creature in the Hindu faith. In retrospect it might have been more sensible if we had taken him as after only 10 days travelling, I was bitten by a rather fierce looking dog, which the locals suspected may have been rabid. We returned to Delhi after a gruelling 35 hour train journey from Pushka, home of the potentially rabid dog. After being examined by a doctor and told about the weekly routine of injections I had to have administered, we decided to fly home and go to The Lakes instead. I am sure that if Worms had come to India with us we would have been able to scare away the very scary dog.

Anyway, back to Thailand. Within the first few days of arriving on Koh Pahngan I had a close encounter with a snake in my bedroom, therefore spent most of the 3 days before the retreat away from my room. I had booked myself into a small hostel about 2 miles away from the monastery and it was very cheap and cheerful. The snakes were especially cheerful with all us juicy Westerners to bite. I consoled myself by grabbing willing, and not so willing tourists to be back-ends, and got them to take ridiculous pictures of Worms doing silly things, such as wading in the sea and lounging on hammocks.

I arrived at the monastery in a bit of a shaky state, recovering from another close encounter with a snake very early that morning. In fact I had left the room at the break of day as I had met the new snake coming in through my uncovered window. It may well have been the same snake as before, or at least a close relation. As I am no snake expert it was difficult to tell, but I certainly didn't like the look of his tongue.

The silence began within the first few hours of meeting the other retreatants. We each had a small, very basic, hut-like room to ourselves; well initially I thought I had a room to myself. Within a couple of days I discovered that I did have a roommate, a very tiny, very yellow scorpion called Cyril. I named him Cyril because somehow this made the whole situation slightly more bearable. No insult intended to any Cyrils out there but for some reason when I think of Cyril I think of a kind elderly Uncle, not a scary yellow scorpion.

Because of my strict boarding school upbringing there was no way I was going to break the silence rule so Cyril and I lived in perfect harmony for 20 days. Worms was a terrific help as I used her to block Cyril's hole. When I realized Cyril was no longer using his hole and was in fact sitting on the ceiling, Worms created a beautiful fur-lined environment for me to sleep on and extra protective bedding at night.

The retreat went surprisingly smoothly and I realised from the outset that it would have been hugely inappropriate to wander around dressed as a cow during the silence. It would have been impossible to find a back-end anyway. However the thought of the wandering Worms and the stir it might have caused, cheered me up when it was all getting a bit too serious, and when Cyril started to get on my nerves, bless his swishy sting. I did have a very giggly moment during the retreat when I realised, after a visit to the interesting Thai style loo, that I had been wandering around for a few hours with my dressed hitched high up into my knickers. I had to go and lock myself in with Cyril for a while just to calm down my hysterical fit of giggles. Cyril did have his uses. It was reminiscent of the time about a year earlier when I had been on a retreat in England at Gaia House. For some reason they had decided to give us very long spaghetti to eat during the very serious silent retreat and the sight of people silently and seriously slurping their very messy, wiggly spaghetti was more than I could bare. I had to go and lock myself in a loo for at least half an hour to try and calm down. I could have done with Cyril in that particular instance.

At the end of the retreat, when the silence was over, I did get Worms out of her bag and took some lovely pictures of the pantomime cow and Buddhist nun outside the Monastery. I think the retreatants and the nuns enjoyed meeting the cow. After quite a heavy going few days it felt good to bring some lightness and laughter into the atmosphere.

On my journey back from Thailand to the U.K I made a stop over in Hong Kong. The main purpose of this little detour was to visit Jamie, who had been Worms' original, and very loyal backend. Within the first couple of days in Hong Kong city I saw a large billboard featuring a pantomime cow with amazing glowing nostrils cavorting with a Chinese dragon. I knew this could have been Worms, and I had a few brief twinges of jealousy and regret, particularly when the nostrils seemed to taunt me with their strategic flashes. The unpleasant and slightly sinister feelings were only fleeting, probably because I'd spent most of the previous two weeks meditating and had managed to reach a slightly higher spiritual pasture.

The higher spiritual dimension that I'd been floating on soon drifted off into the ether as I endured a week of non-stop partying. It was really terrific ! Jamie now managed a chain of nightclubs and restaurants in Hong Kong and I spent the week sampling these different venues, and meeting Jamie's friends. We took some great pictures of Worms enjoying the ambience at Hong Kong harbour.

I arrived back in the U.K feeling as if I'd just disembarked from a yoyo, and I don't mean the aeroplane! It had been a month of contrasts, floating from the serenity of the monastery to landing with a bump into the madness of Hong Kong city. It was now time to return to normality; to settle down, have a nice cup of tea, and put the smelly cow into the washing machine.

Opposite page:

Top: Cow in the South
China Sea, 1996
Bottom: On Kon Pangan,
1996

This page:

Top: Relaxing in
a hammock
Right: Snake alert!
Taken with a
Self Timer at day break

This page:

Top: Cow and nun in
perfect harmony
Right: At Wat Kow Tum, 1996

Opposite page:

Top: Monks at Wat Kow Tum
Bottom: Jamie and Worms in
Hong Kong, 1996

Opposite page:

Top: Out on the town in Hong Kong, 1996
Bottom: Afloat in Hong Kong Harbour, 1996
(Spot the naughty foot!)

This page:

Monica and Bart
feeling calm after
the retreat, 1996

Travels with my Cow 67

Arty-Farty, Makey-Crafty Supercow

Too lethargic to move. Excess of booze last night – well two glasses of wine, but they were quite big. Suddenly I am seized by a surge of creativity and a tingling feeling in my udder regions all at the same time. SUPERCOW arrivée (in French designer type accent) – Arty-farty, I can makey my own clothesees Supercow. I float on my magic sewing basket to my ever-so artistic artistes studio set-up, with designer super-huge sewing machine, looms and other felt-making, tie-dye batique making equipment. On the walls are hung my huge fantastical canvasses-wow, ever-so contemporary. There is no other cow as artistic as me. Scenes of splodges very skilfully and expertly splodged with each splodge in just the right place, and my perfect and most revered work: The Friesian Splodge. Sculptures are on display throughout Le Studio all made from triple recycled driftwood.... and other natural fibres of course. They too have a splodge type theme, though a couple look suspiciously udder-like.

I get to work with my humungous palette. Of course I make my own paints and dyes in a wide range of brilliant hues. My clothes are just to die for too, and when I have finished a petite oil painting, a birthday present for a friend (I make all my own presents of course) I rustle up two cute little outfits for my little cowlets.

All the mothers at school are held spellbound by the outfits that I produce, for fancy dress parties, nativity plays, Hanukah spiels etc., etc. In fact I have just designed an incredible reversible outfit so that the child can appear as two characters at the same party. Wow, I could make a fortune selling some of these clothes but I am far too modest and humble... and kind, and prefer to just get on and do things in my own quiet way with the occasional favour for those who ask. At the moment I am working tirelessly on costumes for an entire primary school's end of term show, and I am completing a hand dyed silk wedding dress for a second cousin. I take great pleasure in my work and am definitely a no stress no mess kind of cow. After a satisfying couple of hours work I float home on my hand-woven magic carpet, just in time for a little meditation and yoga before picking the kiddies up from school.

The Bodhi Tree
Adapted from the original by Nat Needle
(It has a great tune!)

There's old Buddha sittin' under the Bodhi Tree,
There's old Buddha, mind as quiet as it can be
Sittin' like a wise old frog
Sittin' like a lump on a log
Sittin' with a smile on his face
Sittin' like empty space,
Doesn't mind rain, doesn't mind thunder
What could bother old Buddha I wonder

Cows? (use any other word such as 'ice cream'
to show how calm Buddha was)

He wasn't bothered by cows
He wasn't bothered by cows
He let old cows just float on by

Moovin On Up

...Moovin On Out?

I graduated with a BSc in Occupational Therapy in 1998. Worms came to the graduation ceremony with me and some confused business studies student got to be the back end. Shortly after this Dan and I were married and for some reason married life has meant a bit of a change in direction for Worms, Snailey and myself. To a certain extent it was time to put down the udders, and get out the breasts.

The cows weren't present at the birth of my two sons, though I had considered it as a possibility before Jonah was born. This was before I realized what extreme agony I would be in. I had been warned, but of course you don't really believe it until you experience it. All those who have been there, and those who have watched, will realize why the last thing I fancied doing was slinging on my cow suit and doing a jolly little creation dance.

The cows and I have danced at a few weddings and made surprise appearances at birthday parties, in between parental and wifely duties. I've also instigated secret and very anonymous carol singing trips, and mysterious appearances at my boys' primary school. All these activities have been rather middle aged, but I suppose that what happens to older cows rapidly approaching their menopause.

When the kids were both weaned my udders began to get twitchy. I had the inspired idea to start a singing telegram company, combining two of the main loves of my life, singing and my pantomime cow. I could have included another love of my life, my beloved husband as the back end of the singing cow, but singing is really not his thing and he is a particularly irritating back end, a bit like a back seat driver but in a cow. I then 'trialled' him as the front end but this was too unpleasant, especially after a meal of beans on toast!

I had my own business cards printed and sent out loads of press releases to local papers. The press showed some interest and I managed to secure sponsorship from the local fancy dress shop. They offered to lend me any fancy dress outfit I needed, in case people didn't want a singing cow and preferred a singing Batman instead. In return they got coverage in all my press and publicity. I even had my own singing telegram outfit made, complete with jingly bells and a birthday cake hat. It must have looked very silly but my kids thought it looked great, and of course what could be more important?

Surprisingly there seems to be very little call for singing telegrams in The West Country, where we were now living. Despite countrywide publicity, I only received one booking, and that was from a friend for her parents' wedding anniversary. I wore my birthday suit (ho! ho!) and felt much more exposed than being hidden under a nice cosy cow. I sang a happy anniversary song composed especially for the occasion. They enjoyed it, but I certainly felt very silly and preferred being a cow. Shortly afterwards I had two last minute bookings for birthday parties as both singing telegram and cow. This was equally taxing as they were both 6-year-old boys' birthdays. When I arrived in my birthday cake costume, in both instances the birthday boys hid. I then tried to provide some sort of entertainment, which wasn't altogether successful. The boys took great delight at pulling at the cow's tail and I had to coax an unwilling parent to be the back end on both occasions.

More recently I've taken Worms and Snailey into schools and we've done a couple of 'If I were a pantomime cow' workshops in which I've told the story of my travels and the kids have come up with their own ideas of where they'd like to go in their cow suits. Some of the pictures and the ideas have been terrific, and once I get my geography sorted out and stop confusing maps of Europe with maps of The World, they might be quite informative too. I'm now on track to do an all singing, cow-dancing slide show to Women's Institute groups in which I hope to get everyone leaping around in cow suits, inspired by my unique cow-based slide show.

Anyway, enough of this self-promotion and on to the self-analysis. At the beginning of the book I posed the question I am most frequently asked: Why did you travel worldwide dressed as a pantomime cow? And I hoped that in the writing of this book I would come up with a few answers.

When recounting my adventures and browsing over the photos it became clear that the main reason I took the cows with me was because I really enjoy making people laugh, and laughing myself, and the cows make this very easy. My pre-cow travels had been a voyeuristic experience, and apart from the times when I was actually in employment, I was just an observer. Travelling with Worms gave me a sense of purpose as I felt I was able to entertain people and make them laugh, whether they were observers or back-ends.

After nearly twenty years with the cows, I feel ready to move on to something a bit different. It has become increasingly difficult to find willing back ends and my powers of persuasion are getting weaker as I am getting older. My latest idea has been to purchase a barrel organ and to go round houses and streets in Bridport entertaining people with its jolly repertoire. I have become a member of BOGA, the British Organ Grinders Association and am now on the look out for a cheap and cheerful organ. Perhaps when I retire I can travel further afield with it. Maybe the kids will come with me and dance around in the cow suits while I play my tunes. So keep your ears to the ground for the publication of my next book, Travels With My Organ!

Jane and Dan's wedding, 1998

Above: Graduation, 1998

Above: Walditch,
Christmas 2003

Left: Walditch,
Christmas 2004

Above: Primary School
Christmas party, 2005

Right and
following page:
Pictures drawn
by children in
Class 2L,
Bridport Primary
School, 2005

The following pictures
were drawn with the
theme of: "If I was
a Pantomime Cow
I would..."

"...visit Lundon. I would go to the Lundons
Nachrorall Histree Myusem." By Amelia, aged 7

Top: "...like to visit London to visit the Queen." By Katie, aged 6

Middle: "...Like to visit oclglaye" (?!) By Charlie, aged 6

Middle (image in background): "...visit Turkey and go to the Waterpark." By Polly, aged 6

Bottom: "...visit Holland and ride a bike. Moo!" By Nadia, aged 6

TELEGRAM SERVICE: Jane Silver with her children Jonah, aged two, and Toby, seven months, with Worms the cow. **Pictures by David Bendell.**

WHITE STUFF: Jane dressed as Worms the cow on a skiing holiday with her family in France.

Singing cow moo-ves on to pastures new

Report by Simon Peevers

A SOMERSET mum is moo-ving into an udder line of work – as a singing cow.

Former drama student Jane Silver, aged 35, of Coombe St Nicholas, is hoping to milk it by starting up her own singing telegram service.

She dresses up as characters ranging from Worms the cow, a singing carrot and even Dolly Parton.

But she says that going the full monty would be completely beyond the pail.

She said: "I'm not taking my clothes off. Some people have asked me if it is a stripogram but it certainly isn't.

"I have been bringing up the children for a while and I felt like it was time to do something a bit different.

"I decided to use my performance skills and I have a pantomime cow which I picked up when I was working in a theatre years ago which has since been all around the world with me.

"So I came up with the idea of a singing telegram for people's birthdays, anniversaries or any occasion which can be specifically about the person receiving it."

Jane not only has bags of energy and a wide range of costumes but is also a semi-professional singer who has performed with the Wessex Women Choir.

She said: "At the moment I am still making some of the costumes and I will not be starting business until October.

"I will have a carrot costume, the cow and a Dolly Parton character but I can get other costumes if people want something more specific."

After drama school Jane went travelling and took Worms the cow with her – making it the world's best-travelled pantomime cow.

She said: "We used to get dressed up in the cow costume and walk around temples in Indonesia and all over the place.

"People seemed to love the cow so I thought it would be good to use it to entertain people."

Jane's venture is backed by Party On, a fancy dress and costume shop in Station Road, Taunton, which will supply her with costumes.

For bookings in the Chard and Ilminster area from October call 01460 239102.

UDDER BUDDIES: Jane and Worms

Top press stories!

□ **ANIMALS ON CALL:** Carol singers raise money for charity. Picture: JOHN GURD B2134

How the udder half

Panto cow comes a Christmas calling in village

A MYSTERIOUS pantomime cow has again been trudging the streets of Walditch calling on unsuspecting villagers and mooing a variety of festive tunes with live musical accompaniment.

Calves, chickens and tigers, also known as Walditch children from Uplands, also joined in the fun.

One chicken noted that singing in the streets of Walditch was the next best thing to the stable in Bethlehem.

The panto cow and assorted farmyard and jungle animals are keen to retain the air of mystery and remain anonymous.

During the evening they sang carols at the Hyde Residential Home and in the village raising more than £30 for Action Aid, the charity that sponsors children in developing countries.

□ **A MOO MOO HERE AND A CLUCK CLUCK THERE:** Farmyard animals sing carols at the Hyde residential home at Walditch
Picture: JOHN GURD B3055

Village gets in animal spirit

A COUPLE of pantomime cows and a few chickens entertained the residents of Walditch with a medley of different carols.

The farmyard animals sang a different carol at every house to raise as much money as they could for Action Aid.

The lead cow, who wants to remain anonymous, said the evening went very well and the collecting tin was crammed full.

"We gave people shaky eggs to play along to the carols with and tried to sing a different carol at each house. To be honest I was expecting people to find it funnier than they did, but I think it was tea time," said the cow.

Useful Cow, Singing and Writing Contacts

Jane Silver-Corren – contact to arrange to see a light-hearted talk, with slides, songs and dressing-up, on the subject of travelling with a pantomime cow. Tel: 01308 459320

Kate Chidley – For fantastic illustrations of most things especially cows, including copies of all the Supercow illustrations in this book. Tel: 07767 454768

British Trust Conservation Volunteers – Working holidays in the U.K and abroad. Tel: 01302 5722244 (You might even find a Great Bustard!)

Send a Cow – Charity that enables the provision of livestock to developing countries. Tel: 01225 874222

WAWA – Local charity that supports under-privileged communities in Peru. Tel: 01308 485207

The Quangle Wangle Choir-Community choir based in Weymouth, open to all, that encourages members to have fun through singing. Creche also available. Choir Leader Juliet Harwood. Tel: 01305 814940

Natural Voice Practitioners Network-Organisation that encourages use of the natural voice through singing, regardless of musical experience or ability. Has a large number of voice teachers and community choirs nationwide. www.naturalvoice.net

Dorset Literature Network – Local network that supports new and experienced writers. Contact Josie Hickin, Literature Development Officer. Tel 01305 228528